Desert Animals

by Sonya Newland

A+

Smart Apple Media

Published by Smart Apple Media
P.O. Box 3263, Mankato, Minnesota 56002

Printed in the United States of America at Corporate Graphics,
in North Mankato, Minnesota.

Published by arrangement with the
Watts Publishing Group Ltd., London.

Library of Congress Cataloging-in-Publication Data
Newland, Sonya.
 Desert animals / by Sonya Newland.
    p. cm. -- (Saving wildlife)
 Includes bibliographical references and index.
 Summary: "Discusses desert animals around the world and the ways in which they adapt to the desert ecosystem. Introduces
endangered species and conservation efforts and suggests ways for readers to contribute. Includes maps, diagrams, and reading
quiz"--Provided by publisher.
 ISBN 978-1-59920-655-4 (library binding)
 1. Desert animals--Juvenile literature. 2. Wildlife conservation--Juvenile literature. I. Title.
 QL116.N49 2012
 591.754--dc22

                    2010027172

Produced for Franklin Watts by
White-Thompson Publishing
Series consultant: Sally Morgan
Designer: Clare Nicholas
Picture researcher: Amy Sparks

Picture Credits

1019
3-2011

9 8 7 6 5 4 3 2 1

Contents

Words in **bold** are in the glossary on page 31.

What Is a Desert?

A desert is any large area that receives less than 10 inches (25 cm) of rain a year. Deserts cover around a quarter of our planet—and they are growing bigger all the time.

Desert Landscapes

Deserts can be sandy or rocky. Often deserts are located between mountains, and the water that flows from the mountaintops feeds a little moisture into these dry regions. In some deserts, the wind blows the sand into **dunes** hundreds of yards (meters) high. In others, the wind wears away the rock, leaving huge pillars and arches.

Hot desert

Cold desert

Bighorn sheep
(page 10)

North America

Red-kneed tarantula
(page 22)

South America

Life in the Desert

Compared to other **habitats**, deserts have very few animals and plants, but some creatures have **adapted** amazingly well to the harsh environment. Some people even live in deserts, often in places called **oases**, where there is a source of water. Desert peoples include Australian Aboriginals, the San Bushmen of the Kalahari, in Southern Africa, and the Bedouin of the Middle East.

Hot and Cold Deserts

Most deserts are found in Africa, Asia, and Australia. During the day, glaring sunshine heats up the ground, making deserts extremely hot. At night, the temperature drops because there are no clouds to prevent the warm air from escaping. Not all deserts are hot and dry, though. The Gobi Desert in Mongolia is a cold desert, where temperatures during the day can drop far below freezing. The areas around the North and South poles also have very little rainfall. They are sometimes called frozen deserts.

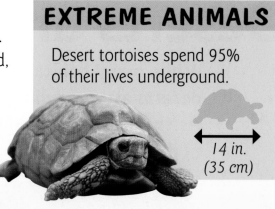

EXTREME ANIMALS

Desert tortoises spend 95% of their lives underground.

14 in. (35 cm)

Saharan addax (page 10)

Bactrian camel (page 8)

Europe

Asia

Tropic of Cancer

Africa

Equator

Australia

Tropic of Capricorn

Desert elephant (page 9)

Bandicoot (page 12)

Deserts under Threat

While many habitats are shrinking, some deserts are spreading into surrounding areas. As this happens, people who live on the edges of deserts are forced to move away.

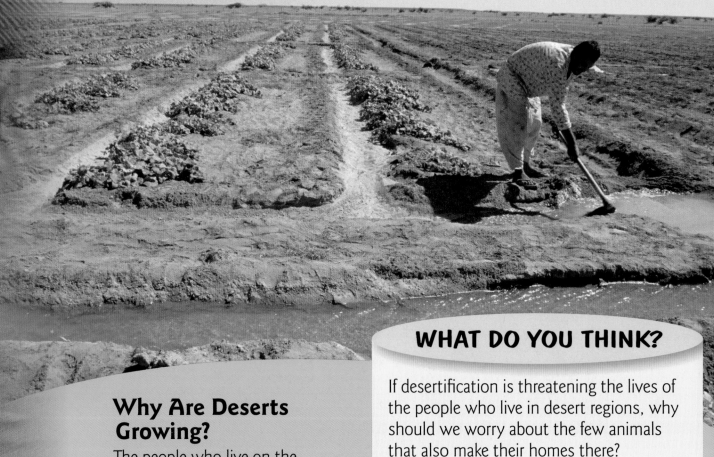

Precious water sources are diverted to help grow crops.

WHAT DO YOU THINK?

If desertification is threatening the lives of the people who live in desert regions, why should we worry about the few animals that also make their homes there?

Why Are Deserts Growing?

The people who live on the grasslands that surround deserts graze their **livestock** there. As the animals reduce the plant cover, the soil gets drier and the top soil blows away. This means that fewer plants can survive. Gradually, the deserts spread in a process called **desertification**. **Global warming** is also causing desertification. Growing deserts might seem like good news for the creatures that live there, but any changes to the environment can badly affect desert animals.

What Else Is Threatening Animals?

Nuclear testing is often carried out in deserts because large areas are uninhabited. This can poison the soil so animals cannot survive. Mining for oil and **minerals** is also damaging desert habitats.

Saving Desert Wildlife

Some of the rarest animals in the world live in the desert **ecosystem**, but they find it hard to survive as the deserts change. If a **species** dies out, others might become threatened because all living things are connected in a "web of life." People now realize how important it is to help desert wildlife.

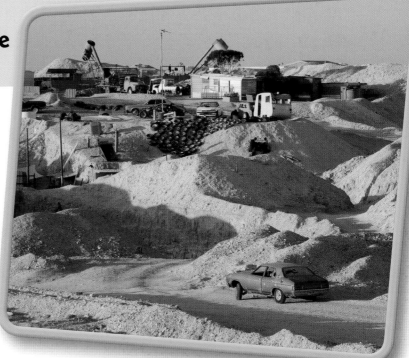

In the Australian desert, people mine for precious opals, which damages the land.

ENDANGERED ANIMALS

The International Union for the Conservation of Nature (IUCN) lists animals according to how **endangered** they are.

Extinct: Died out completely

Extinct in the wild: Only survive in captivity

Critically endangered: Extremely high risk of becoming **extinct** in the near future

Endangered: High risk of becoming extinct in the wild

Vulnerable: High risk of becoming endangered in the wild

Near threatened: Likely to become endangered in the near future

Least concern: Lowest risk of becoming endangered

Large Mammals

Not many big creatures live in the desert. They cannot stay cool enough in the heat of the day or warm enough at night. But a few large animals have found ways to survive.

Saving Camels

Although camels are the best-known desert animals, in fact there are only a few wild camels left. All dromedaries (with one hump) have been **domesticated**, and only around 1,000 wild Bactrian camels (with two humps) survive in remote parts of the cold deserts of Mongolia and China. The areas where they roam have been made into **reserves**, so their habitat is protected. The Wild Camel Protection Foundation has started a **captive-breeding** program in the hope of increasing wild camel numbers in the near future.

▼ *The fat in a Bactrian camel's humps breaks down to release water into its body, so it can go a long time without drinking.*

▼ Desert horses only breed during the rainy season when there is more food, so their foals have a chance of survival.

Desert Elephants

In Namibia and Mali, in Africa, the last remaining desert elephants travel long distances to find water. Threatened by hunting and drought, desert elephants are being helped by organizations such as Save the Elephant. The herds are carefully tracked and monitored, and special watering holes are made for them. Tourism is also helping, as people will pay to see these rare animals and often take part in their **conservation**.

▼ Desert elephants can go for much longer without water than other types of elephants.

Sheep and Antelope

Many different types of sheep and antelope live in deserts all over the world. They are very agile, so they can move around easily in rocky desert landscapes. Some can go for months without drinking water.

Bighorn Sheep

In the United States, desert bighorn sheep have come under threat because people are grazing livestock on the land the sheep once used. This means there is less food for the sheep. They are protected by the **Endangered Species Act**, so they cannot be hunted or killed. This has resulted in an increase in their numbers to around 20,000.

▶ *Overgrazing, hunting, mining, and a reduction in water supplies placed the desert bighorn sheep under threat in the United States.*

SAVING WILDLIFE

Saharan Addax

The addax of the Sahara, in north Africa, is one of the most endangered desert species, with only around 500 left in the wild. Farmers kill the addax because they eat plants the farmers want for their livestock. Although addax are a protected species, they are still hunted illegally for their unusual twisted horns. Zoos in several countries are breeding addax to prevent them from dying out.

Arabian Oryx

Fifty years ago, Arabian oryx were extinct in the wild. Captive-breeding programs stopped them from dying out altogether, and in 1990, the first Arabian oryx was released into the wild. Although still endangered, there are more than 1,000 wild oryx and thousands more in zoos and reserves.

▼ *There are now wild populations of the Arabian oryx in countries including Oman, in southwest Asia.*

WHAT DO YOU THINK?

In 2003, the Arabian Oryx Sanctuary in Oman was taken off the list of **World Heritage Sites** because the government had allowed oil drilling there. What effect might the drilling have on the endangered animals in the sanctuary?

Outback Animals

A group of animals called marsupials lives in the deserts and scrubland of Australia. These creatures, which include kangaroos, wallabies, and bandicoots, carry their young in a special pouch.

Adaptable Marsupials

Some desert **marsupials** have adapted well to their hot habitat. Kangaroos, for example, will dig into the earth and lie on the colder sand beneath the surface to keep cool. Many smaller animals are **nocturnal**, only coming out at night. However, not all marsupials are coping with the changes to their desert environment.

EXTREME ANIMALS

A newborn kangaroo is so tiny that it could fit into a teaspoon. ↔ ¾ in. (2 cm)

Bandicoots under Threat

Around half the 20 types of bandicoot in Australia are endangered. Some, such as the pig-footed bandicoot, are already extinct. To stop this from happening to others, several zoos are taking part in programs that include captive breeding, habitat management, and controlling the **predators** that kill bandicoots, such as **feral** cats.

▶ *Conservation efforts are saving Australia's bandicoots from becoming even more endangered.*

Action Plan for Mulgaras

Mulgaras are important to the desert ecosystem because they keep numbers of some insects and rodents under control. The government's Action Plan for Australian Marsupials and Monotremes includes recovery programs for the endangered mulgara. The plan involves monitoring populations, reintroducing them to areas where they have died out, and educating local people about the importance of saving them.

SAVING WILDLIFE

Bilby

There were once two species of bilby, but one is now extinct and the other endangered because of changes to their environment. There are many conservation efforts to protect bilbies as part of the National Recovery Plan organized by the Australian government. In Queensland, the bilby has even replaced the Easter bunny to help make people aware of its plight!

▼ *The greater bilby is the last of its kind. Captive breeding has resulted in some bilbies being released back into the wild in the past few years.*

Small Mammals

Small animals find it easier than large ones to survive in the desert extremes. They can dig beneath the surface of the soil or sand to escape from the hot sun. Some have even adapted special body features to keep them cool.

Desert Burrowers

Desert rodents, such as kangaroo rats and gerbils, survive the glaring heat of the day by sheltering in burrows. Meerkats live in **colonies** in long underground tunnel networks with several entrance holes.

▼ *Meerkats are sociable creatures and can live in colonies of up to 50 animals.*

EXTREME ANIMALS

Meerkat colonies in the Kalahari Desert in southern Africa set look-outs outside their burrows to warn others when predators are coming their way.

12 in. (30 cm)

Keeping Cool

Animals such as jackrabbits and jerboas have large ears. As warm blood flows into their ears, the heat is lost and the cooler blood returns to their bodies. Fennec foxes in the Sahara have pale fur that reflects the sun to keep them cool, and desert squirrels use their bushy tails as sunshades during the day.

▲ *Small desert **mammals**, such as fennec foxes, often have large ears, which capture breezes and help cool the blood as it circulates.*

▶ *The rare long-eared jerboa was only caught on camera for the first time in 2007.*

Desert Reptiles

Animals such as snakes and lizards can cope with the extremes of heat and cold in the desert better than mammals because their bodies adjust well to the temperature of their surroundings.

◁ *Some desert snakes, such as this rattlesnake, move in a special way called "sidewinding," which leaves only a small part of their body on the hot sand at a time.*

Snake Survival

Many different snakes can be found in the desert, from large boas to tiny vipers. They are plentiful because they can live without a lot of food and water. When food supplies are low, snakes become inactive. Their body digests very slowly so they can last until their next meal. Snakes suffer when numbers of their small mammal prey drop, so snake conservation is often part of wider habitat protection, such as the Sonoran Desert Conservation Plan in North America.

◀ ***Reptiles***, *such as the North American chuckwalla, often stay underground at night and lie in the sun during the day to warm their cold blood.*

Dancing Lizards

In the hottest parts of the world, large and small lizards can be seen basking in the sun. Some, such as the shovel-snouted lizard, protect themselves from the hot sand by doing a special dance, in which they lift two of their feet at a time off the ground. Although some lizards are plentiful, others, including the flat-tailed horned lizard, are threatened because their habitat has been destroyed.

▲ *Flat-tailed horned lizards are now protected by law, as they only survive in a very small part of the North American desert.*

▼ *There are thought to be a few thousand wild gila monsters now, but they are still carefully protected.*

SAVING WILDLIFE

Gila Monster

The gila monster of the Sonoran Desert is one of only two poisonous lizards in the world. Farming has threatened its habitat, but these large lizards are also popular as pets. They were given legal protection in 1952, and since then they have been bred in zoos to preserve their numbers.

Desert Amphibians

Deserts are not an ideal home for animals such as frogs, toads, and salamanders. Although they live on land, they need to lay their eggs in water—and pools of water do not last long in the world's hot deserts.

Adaptable Amphibians

Desert frogs and toads have learned to make the most of water when it appears. They act quickly after rain, laying their eggs in the rainwater pools as soon as they have formed. Their tadpoles then have a chance of changing into frogs before the pools dry up. Endangered frogs, such as the desert rain frog of southern Africa, are being monitored by organizations such as the IUCN (see page 28) because their habitat is being lost and there are concerns about their falling numbers.

EXTREME ANIMALS

The Australian water-holding frog can survive without water for seven years by wrapping itself in a transparent cocoon.

2 ¾ in. (7 cm)

The poisonous Sonoran Desert toad eats small mammals, reptiles, and insects.

Summer Sleeping

Toads, such as the spadefoot toad and the Sonoran Desert toad, survive the harshest season in the desert by sleeping through it. They go into a type of hibernation called **estivation**, where their body temperature drops and their breathing slows down. Many **amphibians** in this area are at risk, but the Sonoran Desert Conservation Plan is finding ways to protect the desert environment and save the endangered amphibians within it.

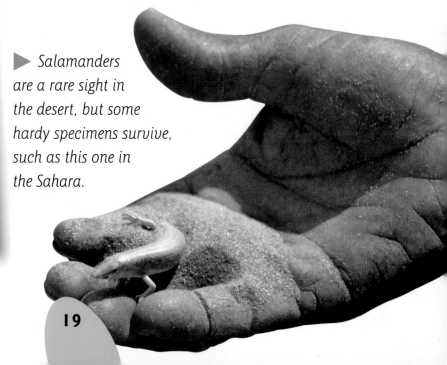

Salamanders are a rare sight in the desert, but some hardy specimens survive, such as this one in the Sahara.

19

Amazing Insects

From busy ants and noisy crickets on the ground to flitting moths and buzzing wasps in the air, there are more types of insects in the desert than any other creature.

Insect Survival

Many insects have a tough outer layer that keeps moisture in their bodies. Their small size also means they can find shelter from the glaring sun. Creatures such as beetles often have long legs to keep their bodies off the hot sand and hard outer wings to stop them from losing moisture.

EXTREME ANIMALS

The fog beetle stands on its front legs and collects moisture that has gathered on its body from fog. It then channels the water down grooves in its legs and into its mouth to drink.

20

Fat Ants

Honey-pot ants have developed an unusual way of surviving during long periods without rain. When a shower comes, they eat up as much nectar as they can from the blossoming flowers and store it in their abdomen, which swells up like a pot. When there is no food in the dry season, the ants release the nectar to feed the others in their colony.

▲ *When full of nectar, honey-pot ants grow so big that they cannot move.*

The Importance of Insects

Insects are vital to the desert ecosystem. They are an important part of the food chain because they are eaten by many other creatures. Some of them help **pollinate** the plants too, helping new flowers grow and providing food and shelter. Protecting the desert environment as a whole will ensure these little creatures survive to help others.

▼ *Desert locusts in southern Africa can be pests for people who live in dry regions.*

WHAT DO YOU THINK?

Desert locusts have become a threat to the people who share their desert habitat because swarms of them eat plants and crops. The desert people kill them with insecticides and fires. How can people protect their own livelihoods while not killing creatures that play an important part in the natural web of life?

Spiders and Scorpions

Spiders and scorpions are plentiful in the deserts. They are important to the desert ecosystem as both predators and prey.

▶ *White lady spiders of the Namib Desert in Africa tap on the sand to communicate with other spiders.*

Spider Survival

From huge tarantulas and wolf spiders to the small but deadly six-eyed sand spider, **arachnids** can be found all across the world's deserts. Some, such as the white lady spider, live in cool burrows beneath the hot sand. When times get especially tough, they use estivation to survive until rain comes and food is more plentiful.

◀ *The Mexican red-kneed tarantula is near threatened because of its popularity as a pet.*

Deadly Scorpions

Scorpions are among the best-adapted creatures to the desert habitat, and there are more than 30 species of scorpion in the Sahara Desert alone. They can survive in extremely high temperatures, and they lose less water through their bodies than any other desert animal. Most scorpions are nocturnal, coming out at night to prey on insects and spiders, which they attack with the deadly sting in their tails. Like spiders, scorpions may come under threat as numbers of the creatures they eat drop.

EXTREME ANIMALS

The sting from a North African death-stalker scorpion can cause a coma or even death in a human.

▶ *The giant desert hairy scorpion is the largest scorpion in North America.*

6 in. (15 cm)

Birds of Land and Air

Birds have an advantage over other animals fighting for survival in the desert because they can fly long distances in search of food and water. It is also cooler in the air than on the ground.

Birds of Prey

High above the harsh desert landscape, vultures, buzzards, and other birds of prey circle, using their amazing eyesight to spot food far below. There is little shelter in deserts, so the animals on which these birds feast often have nowhere to hide and are easy pickings. The loss of their prey, however, can affect bird populations in desert regions.

SAVING WILDLIFE

Lappet-faced Vulture
Lappet-faced vultures are already extinct in some parts of the world where they once lived. There are still a few thousand in the Sahel region of the Sahara Desert and in parts of the Middle East. Groups including Birdlife International are working with the IUCN to formulate an action plan to stop these birds from moving from vulnerable to endangered on the list of threatened species.

The poison that farmers use to keep predators away from their livestock is killing off lappet-faced vultures.

Big Birds

Some desert birds cannot fly at all. Big birds, such as ostriches and roadrunners, can run very fast across the deserts and scrublands in which they live. They have adapted in special ways. Greater roadrunners have a special patch of skin on their necks, which soaks up the heat and helps them warm up quickly after the cold desert nights. Ostriches don't need to drink at all. They get all the water they need from fat reserves in their bodies, just like camels.

Saving Desert Birds

The loss of some desert areas to human settlement and the use of precious water resources has resulted in a decline in numbers of desert birds such as burrowing owls, wrens, and woodpeckers. The Desert Bird Conservation Plan in North America campaigns for the protection and proper management of habitats in the Mojave and Colorado deserts in which these birds are found.

EXTREME ANIMALS

The ostrich of Africa's deserts and grasslands is the largest bird in the world—up to 9 feet (2.75 m) tall and weighing 330 pounds (150 kg).

▲ *The cactus wren of North America uses the few desert plants, such as cacti, to nest in and to provide it with water.*

25

In the Water

It might seem strange to think of fish in a desert, but in desert oases—and scattered throughout the world's driest regions—are springs, ponds, marshes, and streams, which are home to several fish species.

Fish under Threat

Many desert fish are on the endangered list because local people have diverted precious water sources to **irrigate** crops and to use as drinking water. This means that the pools in which the fish live have grown smaller, and some have dried up altogether. Where water remains, it is often polluted by chemicals that nearby farmers use on their crops.

▼ *Desert pupfish have been threatened by the introduction of new species, such as bullfrogs and crayfish, which kill and eat them.*

¾ in. (2 cm)

SAVING WILDLIFE

Pupfish
The tiny pupfish inhabits the ponds and streams of the deserts of North and Central America. They have been threatened by habitat loss and by the introduction of new species into their waters. Different states have different conservation programs. Although fewer than 40 Devil's Hole pupfish survive in their natural home, for example, more than 200 have been bred in special **aquariums**, which may stop them from dying out.

Saving Desert Waters

The Desert Fish Habitat Partnership is an American group focused on saving desert fish. It works with wildlife agencies to identify the species most at risk. It restores water in places where it has dried up and improves the habitat where it has suffered from drought or the effects of farming and human settlement. There are also visitor centers where people can view the fish. Its action plan across the United States may save many species from dying out.

EXTREME ANIMALS

When desert pools dry up, the lungfish can survive for months buried in a mucus cocoon in the wet mud.

▶ Visitors try to spot the rare pupfish at the Salt Creek desert pupfish habitat in California.

What Can We Do?

People all over the world now realize how important it is to control the spread of deserts and to conserve the precious water supplies that remain there. The animals that live in deserts are often specially adapted to their environment and could not survive elsewhere, so helping conserve their habitat is especially important. Local, national, and international organizations work hard to do this, but there are ways that everyone can help.

Find out More...

WWF *(www.worldwildlife.org)*
This is the site of the largest international animal conservation organization. On this site you can follow links to information on all sorts of endangered animals and find out what WWF is doing to save desert creatures.

EDGE of Existence *(www.edgeofexistence.org)*
The EDGE of Existence is a special global conservation program that focuses on saving what it calls "Evolutionary Distinct and Globally Endangered" (EDGE) species—unusual animals and plants that are under threat.

International Union for the Conservation of Nature *(www.iucn.org)*
The IUCN produces the Red List, which lists all the world's known endangered species and classifies them by how under threat they are, from least concern to extinct. You can see the whole list of endangered animals on the web site, as well as discover what the IUCN does to address environmental issues all over the world.

Convention on International Trade in Endangered Species *(www.cites.org)*
CITES is an international agreement between governments that aims to ensure trade in wild animal species does not threaten their survival. It lists animals that are considered to be under threat from international trading and makes laws accordingly.

U.S. Fish and Wildlife Service *(www.fws.gov)*
This government organization was set up to manage and preserve wildlife in the United States. It helps manage wildlife reserves, including those in desert regions, and makes sure laws that protect endangered animals are properly enforced.

Do More...

Sign a Petition

Petitions are documents asking governments or organizations to take action on something people are concerned about. Some of the organizations opposite have online petitions that you can sign to show your support for their campaigns.

Go to the Zoo

Find out if your local zoo is involved in any captive-breeding programs and visit them to find out more. Just visiting the zoo helps support these important programs.

Adopt an Animal

For a small contribution to some conservation organizations, you get to "adopt" a desert animal. They will send you information about your adopted animal and keep you up to date on all the conservation efforts in the area.

Spread the Word

Find out as much as you can about the threats to desert animals and what people are doing to save them. Then tell your friends and family. The more support conservation organizations have, the more they can do!

Read More...

Desert Habitats
Exploring Habitats
by Paul Bennett
(Gareth Stevens, 2007)

Deserts
World about Us
by Harriet Brown
(Stargazer Books, 2007)

Deserts
Caring for the Planet
by Neil Champion
(Smart Apple Media, 2007)

Deserts: The Living Landscape
Biomes of the World
by Robert Greenberger
(Rosen Publishing Group, 2009)

Desert Animals Quiz

See how much you can remember about desert animals by taking the quiz below. Look back through the book if you need to. The answers are on page 32.

1. How much of earth is covered in deserts?

2. Where could you find a frozen desert?

3. How are humans causing desertification?

4. How many humps does a Bactrian camel have?

5. Where are the last surviving wild camels?

6. How is Save the Elephant helping desert elephants?

7. Why is the Saharan addax under threat?

8. Why was the Arabian Oryx Sanctuary taken off the list of World Heritage Sites?

9. In which desert will you find the long-eared jerboa?

10. What is the name given to desert animals that come out at night?

11. How do some snakes move across hot sand?

12. Why are people afraid of gila monsters?

13. How does the spadefoot toad survive the dry season?

14. Why is the desert slender salamander endangered?

15. Why are insects important to the desert ecosystem?

16. How do honey-pot ants survive the dry season?

17. What type of tarantula is protected by the organization CITES?

18. Why do birds have an advantage over other desert creatures?

19. Why are desert fish populations dwindling?

20. Which organization in the United States is saving desert fish?

Glossary

adapted changed in order to survive in new conditions

amphibians cold-blooded animals that spend some of their time on land and some in water

aquariums special enclosures filled with water for keeping fish in

arachnids animals with eight legs, such as spiders and scorpions

captive breeding when endangered animals are specially bred in zoos or wildlife reserves so that they can then be released back into the wild

colonies groups of animals that live and work together

conservation efforts to preserve or manage habitats when they are under threat or have been damaged or destroyed

desertification the process by which deserts are spreading into the regions that surround them

domesticated tamed by humans; domestic animals are often kept as pets or livestock.

dunes large piles of sand created by the wind

ecosystem all the different types of plants and animals that live in a particular area together with the non-living parts of the environment

endangered at risk of becoming extinct

Endangered Species Act a law passed in America in 1973 to protect animals under threat of extinction by active conservation

estivation when insects or amphibians go into hibernation to survive the dry season

extinct when an entire species of animal dies out so that there are none left on earth

feral animals that have gone back to being wild after being domesticated

global warming the rise in average temperatures around the world as a result of human activity, such as burning fossil fuels

habitat the place where an animal lives

irrigate to water crops by diverting water supplies using channels or ditches

livestock animals kept by people for meat or milk

mammals warm-blooded animals that usually give birth to live young

marsupials types of mammals that carry their young in a pouch on their stomach

minerals substances that occur naturally in the earth that people can use to make many different products

nocturnal coming out at night

nuclear testing experiments with powerful nuclear weapons, often carried out in uninhabited areas such as deserts so they do not harm people

oases areas of a desert where underground water comes close to the surface so plants can grow

pollinate to transfer pollen from one flower plant to another so that it can make seeds and grow into a new plant

predators animals that hunt others for food

reptiles cold-blooded animals that lay eggs and usually have scales or plates on their skin

reserves protected areas where animals can roam free and where the environment is carefully maintained for their benefit

species a type of animal or plant

World Heritage Sites places that are protected because they are considered of special natural or cultural interest

Index

Numbers in **bold** indicate pictures

Quiz answers

1. Around a quarter; 2. At the North or South poles; 3. Overgrazing livestock; 4. Two; 5. Mongolia and China; 6. By monitoring populations and creating special watering holes; 7. Because they are being killed by farmers and hunters; 8. Because the Oman government allowed oil drilling to take place there; 9. Gobi Desert; 10. Nocturnal; 11. Sidewinding; 12. They are poisonous; 13. By estivation; 14. Because the water has been polluted or used up; 15. They are eaten by other animals and they pollinate the flowers; 16. By feeding on the nectar they have stored in their abdomens; 17. Mexican red-kneed tarantula; 18. They can fly long distances in search of food and water; 19. Because their pools have dried up or been polluted; 20. Desert Fish Habitat Partnership.